DON'T SPREAD THE WEALTH

THE WEALTH

HOW TO LEVERAGE THE FAMILY BANKING SYSTEM
TO OWN ALL THE GOLD, MAKE THE RULES,
AND ENJOY GENERATIONAL RICHES

Other Books by Jayson Lowe and Richard Canfield

Keep Taxes Away from Your Wealth

Cash Follows the Leader

Canadians Guide to Wealth Building Without Risk

DON'T SPREAD THE WEALTH

HOW TO LEVERAGE THE FAMILY BANKING SYSTEM TO OWN ALL THE GOLD, MAKE THE RULES, AND ENJOY GENERATIONAL RICHES

JAYSON LOWE

RICHARD CANFIELD

ethos
collective

Printed in the United States of America

Published by Ethos Collective™
PO Box 43, Powell, OH 43065
www.ethoscollective.vip

LCCN: 2023923631
Paperback ISBN: 978-1-63680-250-3
Hardcover ISBN: 978-1-63680-251-0
e-book ISBN: 978-1-63680-252-7

Available in paperback, hardcover, e-book, and audiobook.

The Infinite Banking Concept® and Becoming Your Own Banker® are registered trademarks of Infinite Banking Concepts, LLC.

The Family Banking System is trademark pending in both Canada and the United States, owned by Ascendant Financial Inc.

Any Internet addresses (websites, blogs, etc.) and telephone numbers printed in this book are offered as a resource. They are not intended in any way to be or imply an endorsement by Ethos Collective™, nor does Ethos Collective™ vouch for the content of these sites and numbers for the life of this book.

Some names and identifying details may have been changed to protect the privacy of individuals.

Table of Contents

Part 2: The What

Part 3: The How

Note to the Reader

In the world of personal finance, where most are led to navigate through a maze of debt, taxation, and financial insecurity, a revolutionary concept emerges: the Family Banking System (FBS). This system is not merely a financial strategy; it's a paradigm shift in how you think about, interact with, and grow your wealth. It represents the ultimate act of financial rebellion and empowerment: becoming your own banker.

If you haven't already read *Becoming Your Own Banker* by R. Nelson Nash, we highly recommend it. That book changed the course of our lives and laid the foundation for our own system. You can buy a copy by registering for all of your book bonuses at **DontSpreadWealth.com/bonus**.

Your journey to becoming your own banker begins with a fundamental shift in mindset. Imagine a world where you're no longer working tirelessly only to see your hard-earned money slip through your fingers, captured by banks, taxed by governments, and eroded by inflation. The Family Banking System offers a way out, a way to keep your wealth within your family, growing and protected from external threats. You need to learn to think long-range, meaning three generations past your own.

Through engaging thinking exercises, we invite you to confront uncomfortable truths about your financial health. What percentage of your assets are truly protected from loss or taxation? What percentage of your assets can be converted into cash today without reducing the asset's value and without triggering tax? These questions are not meant to discourage but to illuminate the path to financial independence and security through the Family Banking System.

This book lays out the harrowing reality of the modern financial landscape: a world where the average Canadian family pays a staggering average of 43% of their gross household income in taxes, where every conceivable aspect of life is taxed, and where all levels of government hover over your assets with a giant set of utensils, ready to consume them.

Yet, there is hope. Jayson shares his personal journey of financial transformation, from a conventional homeowner in 2008 burdened with a 40-year mortgage to a person who embraced the infinite banking concept, paid off his home in 2015 (33 years ahead of schedule), and continues redirecting the 396 remaining monthly payments into growing an additional $1.5 million in wealth through his Family Banking System. This narrative is not just a success story; it's a testament to the power of becoming your own banker and controlling HOW you finance all the things you need throughout your lifetime.

The Family Banking System is not a complex web of high-risk investments but is grounded in the proper utilization of the best tool to get the job done, which is dividend-paying whole life insurance policies, ideally with a mutual company. This tool not only shields your wealth from taxes, market volatility, and liquidity risks but also ensures daily, contractually guaranteed growth of cash value. Jayson and Richard demystify dividend-paying life insurance, showing how it serves as the best tool utilized to implement a process ... the Family Banking System, providing a secure foundation for keeping the money in and protecting the Family.

Real-life use cases, such as the story of Allan and Janet Antonio, bring the concept to life. Through their journey from financial uncertainty to securing a prosperous future for their family and future generations, you will see the tangible benefits of implementing the Family Banking System. It's not just about wealth accumulation; it's about creating a legacy of financial wisdom and security.

The Family Banking System, as detailed in this book, is more than a financial process. It's a movement towards reclaiming power over your financial life. It's about breaking free from the cycle of debt, taxation, and financial insecurity. It's a call to action for anyone who dreams of a future where their family's wealth is preserved, protected, and passed down through generations.

By embracing the principles laid out in *Don't Spread the Wealth*, you are not just learning to manage your money; you're learning to transform your life and the lives of your descendants. This book is not just a guide to financial success; it's a blueprint for building a legacy of generational riches.

Control HOW you buy, invest, and borrow throughout your lifetime while increasing your wealth and shielding it from taxation.

It's time to stop being controlled by debt, the banks, and outside factors and to start calling the shots financially in your life.

In this book, you'll discover:

- The most powerful wealth retention process ever developed

- How you can address risk and erroneous taxation and keep both away from your wealth

- Real-life examples of people who have implemented the system

- How you finance your business and everything you need personally without worrying about the banks

- How you can either get started or grow your existing system today

- Take advantage of high-caliber opportunities with ready access capital, on demand and on your terms

- How you can transfer this wealth mentality to future generations over a long period of time

PART 1

The Why

1

Why the Poor Get Poorer

Have you ever heard the expression rags to rags in three generations? According to a Chinese proverb, three generations is how long it takes to lose everything.

The first generation makes the money through wise financial decisions and hard work. The second generation, after seeing the work done by their parents, is able to maintain the wealth. But the third generation, not having seen the labor of the first generation, recklessly spends the wealth, leaving the family back where they started: in rags.

In 1810, Cornelius Vanderbilt started his business by borrowing money from his mother. By the time of his death nearly 70 years later, he was the richest man in the United States, thanks to his steamboat and railroad empires. His son, the heir to his business and fortune, expanded the business, doubling the family's wealth. But the third generation stopped growing the fortune. Instead, they spent it on yachts and estates. Today, the wealth is gone.

Even if you have a solid grasp on how to maintain your wealth, it means nothing if you aren't transferring that knowledge to the next generation through an established system and meaningful, ongoing conversations with your family. In three or fewer generations, everything the preceding family members built can dissipate into nothing, like water draining out of a hole in a bucket.

And just as water is essential to life, money is a necessity in our society. You want to make sure your bucket stays full—not just for yourself, and not just for the next two generations, but for all the future generations of your family.

The Challenges of Intergenerational Wealth

Typically, maintaining generational wealth tends to face three big challenges:

Challenge #1: The assumption that the transfer of wealth only happens upon the death of a parent or grandparent. The truth is, when none of a person's wealth is transferred to the next generation while that person is still alive, they miss out on seeing their legacy in action.

Challenge #2: Wealth transfers can be targeted by people who want to claim that wealth for their own—including tax collectors, creditors, and others who feel they have a right to their share. We believe that wealth belongs in the family, not with anyone else.

Challenge #3: Wealth transfers can happen without any conversation with the generations who will inherit that wealth. Coming into a large sum of money unexpectedly, without a plan in place to manage that money, easily leads to financial disaster. We're sure you've heard the stories: someone wins big in the lottery, and within a few short years, the money is gone, and often, the winner's relationships are tested to the breaking point. The same thing can happen with intergenerational wealth when the inheritors are unprepared. The problem isn't the money—but what they do or don't do with it.

How do you overcome these challenges? The answer is simple: knowledge. And knowledge is exactly what we're here to impart.

The knowledge we will share was lovingly passed to us from our mentor, the late best-selling author R. Nelson Nash. Nelson was the creator of the game-changing Infinite Banking Concept that sits at the core of our financial philosophy.

In December 2017, Jayson envisioned a way to capture Nelson Nash's wisdom before he passed, inspired by a profound sense of gratitude and a desire to preserve Nelson's remarkable essence. Initially conceived as a webinar where Nelson would expand on each chapter of his book, Jayson's discussions with Nelson soon evolved into a documentary film project. This comprehensive deep dive into Nelson's life's work aimed to give viewers a profound glimpse into his exceptional character.

Jayson commissioned the project, inviting Richard as his first collaborator. This sparked something magical. We believed that if everyone could meet Nelson one-on-one, they would feel inspired to take control of their financial lives. Over the course of a week, we worked with Nelson, his son-in-law David Stearns, and a small film crew to capture the incredible wisdom and stories of Nelson, and the profound impact he had on us and the world.

Nelson viewed the film in February 2019, just before his passing in March. In Jayson's last conversation with Nelson, two weeks before his passing, Nelson imparted, "I want you to remember this is all about the message, not the man."

With the Nelson Nash Institute's full support, we believe the documentary film "This is Nelson Nash" truly captures that sentiment.

It starts with mindset.

As Nelson began every live seminar: "You see, it's all about *HOW* you think. It's all about how *YOU* think. It's *ALL* about how you *THINK*."

We are going to teach you the critical mindset to set the stage for you to create a multigenerational financial impact—an impact that allows you to be confident in the current and future success of your family.

At the core of this success is one concept: the Infinite Banking Concept.

What is IBC?

Search "Infinite Banking Concept" on any social media platform, and you'll find endless posts, infographics, and content makers trying to describe what, exactly, IBC is. You'll see financial advisors advertising their "unique" design for a whole life insurance contract, immediately followed by financial academics claiming that IBC is a scam. No one can seem to agree on what IBC is, and whether it works.

The more you scroll, the more lost you'll become. You'll likely end up convinced that the Infinite Banking Concept (IBC) has something to do with choosing the right life insurance policy and knowing the best life insurance companies to buy them from—after all, many, if not most, definitions of IBC focus on the product of life insurance.

> *"Most people have no idea that Infinite Banking Concepts has absolutely nothing to do with life insurance."*
> —R. Nelson Nash

It's absurd.

But here's the truth: IBC actually has nothing to do with life insurance. IBC is a process, a concept that begins with the way you think. And the more you listen to the noise around life insurance contracts, the more you'll end up trying to build a strong financial system on a weak foundation.

So, when we say that IBC is a process, what does that actually mean? Let's start with the B: Banking. We believe the banking system as it is designed today is set up for you to hand all of your money over to someone else who thinks they can do better with it than you can. Banks have established a system of control whereby they are always the first ones to get access to your money. You may believe the money in your bank account is yours, but it isn't. As soon as you deposit money into that account, it becomes the "property" of the bank. Your account balance is actually an IOU statement. You become an unsecured creditor of the bank and they owe you that deposited money on demand.

That's why savings and checking accounts are "liabilities" on a bank's balance sheet, not assets. They pay you very little, if anything, to borrow that money from you—all the while systematically making far more with your money than you do. They place limitations on when and how much you can take out or move around, and they charge you fees for a variety of services, which all involve gaining access to your own money.

Have you ever experienced frustration or limitations in dealing with traditional banks?

That feeling of being just another account number? Lost in a sea of transactions and red tape? Nosey credit applications and borrowing terms that you do not control?

It's easy to see why many believe that, in general, banks are not your friend—especially after the 2008 financial crisis.

But it's also a theme that has been reflected in the media for generations—just think about the beloved Christmas classic *It's a Wonderful Life*. When George Bailey's uncle misplaces money he plans to deposit, the bank's board member keeps it for himself. George tries to take out a loan from the bank to recover the missing funds, but he is denied. Without help from the bank, he faces criminal charges and the loss of his business.

The message of this sequence of events is clear: that banks only have one goal in mind, and that goal is to make as much money as possible for their stockholders—even at the expense of customers (the folks who deposit all the money there). It is, of course, an extreme example; the bank (and the people running it) seems unnecessarily cruel, if not downright evil. Understand, we are talking about those in control of the bank, not the average person who works on the front line.

Chances are, the people running banks are not truly evil or cruel either. But they are people, just like the rest of us, and they're in business with a motive to earn profit (understandably so). And so naturally, they may be inclined to look out for their own best interests. Someone at a bank will simply never look after your interests as well as you will. The problem is not with the person but with the system, which is designed to have control over the use and liquidity of your capital so the banks can profit off of your deposits twenty-four hours a day while paying you a pittance in interest to keep your money there. But what you "think" is there isn't really there. It is all an illusion.

When you deal with a bank, you are handing over your hard-earned money to someone and some organization that may not always be acting in your best interest, even if it's not malicious. When you deposit your money into a bank, all of that financial energy is transferred away from you to the institution, which puts all that money to work for their stockholders (The Bank Owners) instead of for you (The Depositor and The Borrower). Money has to flow. Otherwise, it's worthless.

The Infinite Banking Concept enables you to take control of the banking function as it relates to your needs, to be in a position of total and absolute control over HOW you finance the things you need throughout your lifetime. We want to put you in the driver's seat—and we, along with thousands of our Clients, know firsthand that IBC is the best way to do it. IBC means becoming your own banker by implementing a process that you control. Every dollar that you store inside of your own warehouse of wealth is optimized for your lifespan, so you never give up its earning potential.

"The Infinite Banking Concept is a lifestyle, not a financial plan."—David Stearns, Co-Director of the Nelson Nash Institute

Look at it this way: every buying decision that you make is a financing decision. You will either pay interest to someone else for the privilege of using their money for purchases and spending, or you will give up the interest your money could have earned when you pay cash for things.

Everyone must reckon with that fundamental truth. There are no exceptions.

You either "pay up" or you "give up." IBC involves building your own warehouse of wealth inside of an entity that you own while controlling HOW you finance everything that you need, when you need it, throughout your life. And yes, dividend-paying life insurance policies are the best tool utilized to implement this process—but that is merely the tool.

> *"If you put the best tool for the job in the hands of an incompetent, not only will that person not turn out any good work with the tool, he'll likely break the darn tool."*
> —R. Nelson Nash

IBC is the process itself. You need a good coach to show you how to do this properly.

Selecting the best coach to help you implement this process involves a few critical steps.

First, evaluate the coach's experience, ideally choosing an Authorized Infinite Banking Practitioner. Ask for a substantial sample size of existing client reviews; a Practitioner with 100 or more client reviews typically indicates significant experience. Additionally, request that the Practitioner demonstrates how they are implementing this process in their own life, showcasing real examples rather than just their portfolio of life insurance contracts.

We are proud to showcase our sixteen years of specializing in this process, working alongside a team of 50 amazing, dedicated people (and growing). Our commitment to excellence has earned us over 1,268 five-star Google reviews, and the number is steadily rising. We would love to connect you with the right person on our team to see if we can establish a basis to serve you.

Unlike financial products such as 401k plans, RRSPs, mutual funds, or stock portfolios—which are often presented as more traditional and, therefore, more trustworthy options—IBC is not a product, and it is certainly not dependent on interest rates or the state of the economy. These methods all focus on a hope, wish, and prayer model for their results. Or, as Nelson often said, Wall Street is hooked on a very powerful drug . . . "Hope-ium." Instead, IBC creates a peaceful, stress-free way of life financially because you no longer have to play their game and no more sleepless nights or heart palpitations every time the financial entertainers start talking about the market's volatility.

To build wealth, you've got to reckon with tax risk, market risk, and liquidity risk.

Would you sleep easier at night if you knew that your money was no longer subjected to these risks?

Yes: _____

No: _____

Because IBC is a process and not a product, it requires you to think differently than those who hand control of their money over to institutions that manage 401ks (RRSPs in Canada), mutual funds, stock portfolios, bonds, or even real estate. Thinking differently begins with understanding the problem. Otherwise, the solution won't matter to you.

The problem is you're doing all the work, and everyone else is getting all of your money!

Ask yourself, "WHO is the banker in my life?" Someone must perform that function as it relates to your needs. As Nelson taught us, you can become your own banker, making all the rules and earning the profits. Over time you can stop relying on a conventional bank for anything other than the convenience of debit. And that is a peaceful, stress-free way of life financially.

Borrowing From Your System

Think about it: who makes money when you pay off your loans? You certainly don't. You repay the money you borrowed to the financial institution, then you give them *more* money in the form of interest, and you never see any of the principal or interest again. And neither does any generation that comes after you. You are paying to access someone else's pile of money. Why? Well, they accumulated that pile, and it has value. You always pay for the use of that value. Capital always has a cost.

If you have taxable savings or assets, you have a problem, and so do your beneficiaries. Nelson Nash did an extensive study and found that the average North American paid out 34.5 cents of every disposable dollar in interest. He was not talking about the "rate" of interest. No, he was referencing a much less understood aspect, the "volume" of interest. That is, the actual amount of dollars that will be paid out of cumulative payments on the many debts one acquired over a lifetime. Just consider the first five years of a mortgage contract and think about how much interest is paid out of each individual payment for that 60-month period . . . it's a staggering number!

What are some examples of interest payments that you have had to deal with in your lifespan so far?

Examples: (i.e. credit cards, loans)

_____

_____

_____

_____

Why are you paying others for access to their pile of money? Most likely because you didn't have your own pile of capital to tap into and because you didn't know there was another way. You transfer all your money away from you and permanently give up the opportunity to earn interest on that money, not only for the remainder of your lifetime but for every generation that comes after you. And you repeat that cycle over and over again.

How does that make you feel?

You should discover how to recapture the interest you pay on your loans because it turns the tide financially in your favor. First, you are going to need the best tool to get this job done: a dividend-paying whole life insurance policy or, ideally, a system of policies with an emphasis on high cash value accumulation.

Who is buying the most dividend-paying life insurance? BANKS

So let's mimic what the banks do because we'll do ok!

With a participating whole life insurance policy (or, ideally, a system of policies), you immediately have the contractual authority to request loans against your policy. This is not "borrowing from yourself," a statement you often hear and which is part of the confusion around this process. It is both technically inaccurate and misleading. You are not borrowing from or banking on yourself. **Cash value is not actual money** but rather the net present value of the future death benefit payment. You can borrow against this cash value, using it as collateral, to access actual money from the life insurance company (which you co-own). This allows you to utilize the money without ever interrupting the daily cash value growth of your policies.

Policy loans are immediately accessible by the policy owner. You can borrow against a maximum of 90% of the total cash value (less than any existing loan balance) on demand and on your terms without reducing any of the policy's cash value and without triggering a taxable event.

These policy loans are unstructured, meaning there is no qualifying, no credit check, no income verification, and no repayment schedule. This flexibility is unmatched in the financial world we live in today. The policy owner is in a position of total and absolute control.

What do you mean there is no repayment schedule?

It's quite simple. The life insurance company guarantees the collateral (your cash value) for the loans. When the insured passes away, the total death benefit minus any outstanding loan balance is paid directly to the named beneficiaries. In other words, the life insurance company, which you co-own, views policy loans as an invested asset on their balance sheet. In fact, it is one of the safest investments the life insurance company can make because the return is guaranteed.

It is important to note that when you repay a policy loan, that money flows back to the life insurance company's general fund—and is immediately re-accessible by you or any other captive customer.

Imagine this breakthrough: you are also a "participating" co-owner of this company. This means you share in the divisible surplus generated by the life insurance company in the form of annual dividends. All of your financial energy now flows back into a system you co-own and profit from instead of going to someone else's bank. Yes, I said it again—someone else's bank.

But that's not all. Any interest you pay to the life insurance company you co-own directly contributes to its net earnings. And what's one primary criterion for calculating annual dividends? You guessed it—the contribution principle.

Think of it this way: if you and I co-owned a Safeway grocery store and decided that our annual dividends would be based on how much each of us contributed to the net earnings, would we ever buy our groceries from Walmart? Of course not. We'd want our store to receive all that money so we could buy more groceries to sell to more captive customers.

Think about it. This isn't about interest rates. It's about where your money is flowing to and who it's being put to work for.

As previously mentioned, these policy loans are considered an invested asset on the balance sheet of the life insurance company. And it keeps getting better: while you have the actual money you borrowed, the insurance company you co-own is required to continue growing your total cash value every single day you age due to a significant contractual guarantee, which is the total cash value must equal the total death benefit by age 100 of the life insured in Canada, and age 121 of the life insured in the United States.

That means your total cash value must climb upward daily, uninterrupted by any policy loan balance. You continue earning on the entire total cash value in your system of policies regardless of the loan amount you access for life's needs. And there's also that tax-free death benefit we mentioned thrown in for good measure.

Consider this: you pay zero income tax on the death benefit proceeds, zero tax on the daily buildup of cash value, and zero tax on the annual dividends when used to purchase paid-up additions. Your cash value never decreases, and dividends cannot be repossessed or lose value. You enjoy contractually guaranteed daily growth of cash value and lifetime access to real money, on demand, on your terms, without reducing the asset's value or triggering a taxable event.

In Canada, dividend-paying life insurance contracts are also completely exempt from the passive investment income tax rules that frustrate Canadian business owners. Your corporation can own it, pay the premiums, and fully utilize it.

Policy loans are accessible to you on demand, without any frustrating credit applications or checks, because it is a private loan arrangement. You should implement this process because of the aggravation it will save you from having to deal with someone else's bank. And the best part? You dictate the repayment schedule. You become your own banker, controlling HOW you meet your financial needs. And as a co-owner of the life insurance company itself, you also share in the profits generated year after year, decade after decade.

Knowing all the above, how much of your money do you not want residing here?

These are just the basics—there is even more you can do with this tool to increase your wealth further. Say the insurance company sets a 6% simple interest rate on your policy loan. Rather than repaying the loan at 6%, you can repay it at 10%. The extra 4% interest that you choose isn't actually interest. It's more premium, and the higher your premium, the more capital you accumulate, from which you can keep borrowing against. This also effectively increases your contribution to the net earnings of the life insurance company (that you co-own), which means you, along with every other co-owner, receive a larger share of a larger divisible surplus. In essence, you can always be expanding your capital base by following these simple principles.

Every time you have a need for finance, no matter how big or small, you can request a policy loan provided you have sufficient total cash value as collateral. As you repay the loans on your terms, you are replacing capital you have already used, and each payment is money you can access again at any time and for any purpose. By controlling how you finance your life's needs, you can increase your wealth drastically because you're in a position of total and absolute control.

How does that make you feel?

What happens when you max out your premium inside a single policy? Well, what happens when a bank is profitable in one area of town? They open up more branches in other areas of town! You can expand your system by simply purchasing new policies on yourself, your family members, and even business partners. As Nelson Nash said, "This is meant to be a system of policies." Each policy is like a new branch of the first national bank of you!

This is only a taste of how IBC works. And we know it works well because this system has become our lifestyle for the past sixteen years, controlling how we finance homes, mortgages, education, cars, investments, and our growing companies with people, technology, and equipment.

All along the way, honoring our obligation to pass on this knowledge to you.

Today, the tens of thousands of people who have started this journey have already freed so many future generations from the need for traditional banks for anything other than the convenience of a debit card. But the only thing that truly determines whether those future generations will keep it that way is to continue to pass down the knowledge of how to do so. In other words, don't spread the wealth away from your family. Keep it where it belongs for as many generations as possible.

Generational Wealth Requires Generational Knowledge

The more people you include in your Family Banking System (FBS)™, the more you can expand your family's wealth, which is why it's important to include both immediate and extended family. Together, you can combine your resources and keep each other accountable, creating a profitable system.

But it doesn't stop there. By implementing this process, you are not only improving your family's finances today—you are also building a legacy for your children, grandchildren, great-grandchildren, and beyond, provided you teach them the process. Future generations will pass on the knowledge of the family banking system, giving them the freedom to create the lives they want without having to rely on temperamental markets and creatures of the tax code (i.e. 401K's, RRSPs) to get them through life.

In order to do this, you have to get comfortable with something many people find very uncomfortable: thinking and talking about money.

Thinking Exercise

You are doing all the work, and everyone else is getting all your money. How does that make you feel?

Scale of 1 – 10
1 – Doesn't bother me, it's always been this way
10- I'm furious
Score: _____

What portion of YOUR net worth is completely shielded from any risk of loss or taxation?
0% - 100%
Your % _____

Of all YOUR assets, what percentage can be converted into cash today, without reducing the asset's value and without triggering tax?

Scale of 1-10
1 – No Clue
10 – 100%
Your Score: _____

How many high-caliber investment opportunities have you missed out on because you didn't have ready access to money, on demand, on your terms?

Score 1 – 10
1 – None
10 – More than I can count
Your Score: _____

Money Myths

Most people don't like to talk about money, let alone think about it, so let's start with the things we *do* like to say about money. There is a lot of "common wisdom" out there about money, including some things you likely accept as truth thinking about what they really mean. But many of these "pearls of wisdom" are simply not true.

Take these three chestnuts of common wisdom. Which of these would you say are myths?

- A penny saved is a penny earned.

- Money is the root of all evil.

- Money is a taboo topic.

The answer is: all of them!

In the end, a penny saved is just a darn penny, and money is a medium of exchange. No matter how much money you save, if all you're doing is saving, you will never create true wealth. Why? Because wealth is NOT money. If you're saving money, it's likely for some objective where you have to spend to achieve it. Save, then spend, repeat. You always deplete the balance and have to rebuild it. Every time your account goes down for a spending decision, you have less asset base to earn growth on. This cycle—called lost opportunity cost—is one of the leading wealth killers on the planet.

The myth that money is the root of all evil is based on 1 Timothy 6:10, but the actual meaning of the verse is entirely different than we have come to believe. The verse says, "For the love of money is a root of all kinds of evils." Money itself is just an object —what creates problems is when people *love* money more than anything else. We can view money as so important that we place it above everything else—above family, above community, above being a good person. But money should never be our top priority. Money is sometimes the means by which we fulfill our priorities.

Pro Tip: Take a moment and write down what your top priorities are right now that require the use of money to fulfill. Do not overthink it—write down the first five things that come to mind. You can add to them later, but taking action while you read this book will give you the most value!

These first five things may form part of your action plan for engaging your family in this process to create the generational success you are looking for. Don't put off until tomorrow what can be done today!

My top priorities that require money are:

1. _____

2. _____

3. _____

4. _____

5. _____

Money itself has never been the problem—but not talking about money can lead to serious problems, which is why money should not be a taboo topic. Not talking about money can tighten the grip it has on your life. If you look at it as a taboo topic, you'll never be able to gain the knowledge you need to expand your wealth—and neither will your kids or their kids. In fact, if you have a negative feeling about money or even conversations that surround money, this will show up in a tangible way for your kids and family members. The result often is a negative cycle that perpetuates. You must become the change by making a commitment to reframe this model. Your family and your legacy depend on it.

Break The Cycle

We are going to help you transfer that knowledge so that your financial objectives can become achievable realities.

You will learn how to think beyond your lifespan and set up the proper rules of money engagement for you and your family to follow.

Pro Tip: Use affirmations to help you reset your relationship with money until it becomes second nature. These are examples you can use as inspiration:

- I will think beyond my own lifespan.

- I will set a positive example for my family to follow.

- Whatever I borrow from the Family Banking System, I will repay with interest.

- I know my top priorities. Money is simply a tool for me to fulfill them.

- I embrace generational thinking. What I do through-out my lifetime financially benefits my children.

- My kids will continue my legacy. I want that legacy to be a positive one, and I will show them how.

Remember your values, and you will be aligning with the core of the Infinite Banking Concept. Those who are clear with their values and long-term thinking have the most success long range with this process.

A good man leaves an inheritance for his children's children
- Proverbs 13:22

By implementing what we teach, you're going to have a lasting impact not only on your life, but your children, their children, and every future generation that comes after them. In fact, you will likely impact much more than that. Consider the many foundations that exist that continually provide value to worthy causes. These are clear examples of this mindset in action, cascading over multiple lifespans. With this book, you can build an impact as large as you can dream. After all, there are no unreasonable goals, only unreasonable timelines. When you think beyond your own lifespan, the timeline is infinite!

And it is impossible to place boundaries around "infinite."

Whether it's changing the "wealth is gone in 3 genera-tions" or "rags to rags," each of these cycles starts with you. You are the force of change on your family's financial trajectory.

Here are 3 steps you should take because by doing so:

- You empower yourself with financial independence

- You gain control over your economic future

- You unlock wealth creation that aligns with your personal values and goals

Next Steps:

1. Intentionally build a pool of capital inside an entity that guarantees daily growth of cash value and ready access to money on demand, on your terms

2. Recapture the interest, the money that you pay to banks now and in the future and that you use to finance all the things you need to purchase throughout your lifetime

3. Protect your livelihood, real estate portfolios, investments, retirement account balances, and everything you work for from being decimated at the highest levels of taxation

2

Why the Rich Get Richer

A re you the master of your money, or do you let it master you? Look at a family's financial history, and you can often tell the answer.

Growing up, our families are often our main source of financial information—whether they were anxious about money or spent it recklessly and never had more than a few dollars to spare. As kids learning how the world works, we saw how our parents acted financially and either desired to follow their lead or go in the opposite direction. Their money habits were a byproduct of what they learned from their parents, and so on.

As we age, our relationships begin to shape our perspective on personal finances. Do we perpetuate the financial patterns of previous generations, or do we choose to deviate from traditional methods, whether for better or for worse?

Having witnessed our parents' financial difficulties and challenges, we realized there had to be a different approach.

Our parents, similar to many others, didn't always engage in constructive discussions about money and wealth. It's possible they, like many others, had unhealthy relationships with their finances, whether in abundance or scarcity. In reality it is very likely that our parents had the issue when they were children where conversations about money were either difficult or non-existent. We aim to guide you in reclaiming control and breaking the cycle, as we have. But before we delve into that, it's important to share some of our background.

Hitting Rock Bottom: Jayson's Story

In the early 1970's, my parents purchased their first home for $30,000. My family was one of many affected by inflation skyrocketing in the early 1980's. Interest rates peaked at 21.5% ... IF you were a prime customer of the bank. I've never met anyone who's prime, and my parents were certainly not prime either. I recall seeing a letter arrived with the logo of The National Bank of Canada: a pre-foreclosure notice. I'll never forget the devastated look on my parents' faces as they read the contents.

I grew up as a toddler listening to my parents argue about money all the time. They argued a lot—the same kinds of conversations about money that were happening all over North America, and that still happen today. All my father did in response to the rising costs of living was work harder. They never considered that there may be a better way to not only keep more money in the family but to multiply it and create wealth.

My parents were amazing in so many wonderful ways, but to my knowledge, they never read a book like the one you are reading now. So, rather than being coached through their financial struggles, they ended up separating.

It was in this same period that R. Nelson Nash, then in his early 50s, found himself half a million dollars in mortgage debt. Initially, he had been borrowing at 9.5% and paying $47,500 of interest to service that debt. But then 1982 came along, and the rate peaked at 21.5% for prime customers. Nelson had to pay 1.5% above prime, hitting a devastating 23%. That amounted to an additional $67,500 of interest per year that he wasn't expecting to pay! That number is more than the average North American makes in an annual salary in 2024, 43 years later! This led, of course, to Nelson facing enormous stress and pressure to find a way out of that situation.

Then, as if that wasn't enough, a business partner in a real estate development project bankrupted. Nelson had to eat that partner's share of the deal, which added another $300,000 to his already massive debt load. To give you an idea of the scale, if you factor in inflation from 1981 to 2022, that $800,000 would be equivalent to $2,607,490 in today's U.S. dollars.[1] He had done everything he had been told to do by all the real estate gurus. These gurus all preached "the power of leverage" as the key to wealth in real estate—still what is preached today. However, none of the gurus of that era—or today's—talked about what happens when the interest rate lever goes the other way.

As he saw it, Nelson had only one choice: he could file for bankruptcy. Everyone said, "Nelson, just sell the real estate," and he thought, "What fool is going to buy this from me when interest rates are this high?" As the rates rose, the buyers disappeared, and the value of the real estate was affected.

---

[1]   CPI Inflation Calculator. "$800,000 in 1981 → 2023 | Inflation Calculator." Accessed December 20, 2023. https://www.in2013dollars.com/us/inflation/1981?amount=800000.

This placed him and his family in a precarious position. It wasn't until a difficult 18-month period of personal struggles and late nights of prayer that Nelson realized a different solution was right in front of him. He said it hit him like a two-by-four across the eyes.

Nelson had already been paying a large amount of premium each year for several dividend-paying participating whole life insurance contracts. He realized he could borrow money from the life insurance companies at 5% to 8%. However, he was limited in what he could access because he had not been putting enough money in. His epiphany was that he needed to reverse the flow of money that was going to lenders and direct as much as possible into more policy premiums. He could then, over time, "get rid of those snakes and dragons" by accessing policy loans to pay them off and recapture the interest.

Nelson knew it would be difficult and would take time, but he was committed to getting out of financial prison. After all, the time was going to go by anyhow!

After 13 years, Nelson had finally completed the process and for the remainder of his lifetime, Nelson and his wife, Mary, never saw a commercial bank for anything other than the convenience of debit. All their money stopped flowing away from them and instead flowed back to their family. They kept the flow of payments and financing for mortgages, vehicles, investments, and even airplanes that Nelson owned completely within the family. The steady, ongoing stream of payments never left their family's money pool again.

Robbing the Family of Wealth

My dad worked in the same career for 35 years. Everything we needed to purchase was either paid for in cash or financed by someone else's bank. Both methods involved a permanent transfer of money away from the family. Let this sink in: Our family's monthly debt servicing payments were someone else's passive income.

Is that happening to you?

All our lives while growing up, he transferred money away from his family with every transaction. After he retired, his financial advisor recommended he surrender his whole life insurance policy to get the cash surrender value (something you can still do to this day). After all, the advisor reasoned, my dad still had his pension to act as a nice financial cushion.

But after cashing out his life insurance policy, every day in retirement began to look like a Saturday. My dad squandered his money on a snowmobile, new golf clubs, and other impulse buys. Then, almost a year later, he died suddenly, and with him, any chance of an inheritance.

Financially, all he left his family were problems, not money.

He never received the value of his 35-year pension income as he wasn't around to spend it. It was locked away in a prison that he was never able to use during his working years to support our family. Had he had access to borrow against that pool of money, perhaps we never would have received that heart-wrenching letter from the National Bank.

If my dad had known about the process of Becoming Your Own Banker ®, The Infinite Banking Concept ® early in his career, he could have implemented the Family Banking System (FBS)™ using the money he put into his pension to create a system that was constantly flowing back to us and for future generations. He would have been able to leave his family both the money and the knowledge to continue the system, instead of stress and worries.

Beyond that, when he passed, there would have been something in place to sort through the mess we all leave behind when we go. It wouldn't have changed the impact of his passing, but it would have reduced the stress and created the space and time to grieve properly.

This alone is reason enough to get this system started: so that you and your family do not become another statistic and experience what my sister and I did.

Painful Financial Lessons Create Everlasting Wealth

Nelson and my father aren't the only ones who reached low moments in their financial lives. I, Jayson, had my own a couple of decades back.

Imagine, if you will: It's 2004 in Alberta, Canada, at about 7:30 in the evening. I'm standing in a dark, cold living room. A "for sale" sign is on the lawn, one that isn't there by choice.

Up to that point in my life, I had done everything mainstream financial advisors told me to do. I put money into Registered Retirement Savings Plans (essentially the Canadian equivalent of a 401k plan). I borrowed a lot of the bank's money to buy rental real estate. And yet, instead of the wealth I was promised, I found myself in a desperate situation.

My first marriage had failed. I was deeply in debt. I was on the brink of financial ruin. Where could I go from here?

Fast forward to 2008, when I had the opportunity to attend a three-day conference in Vegas and the topic being taught was what I later learned to be The Infinite Banking Concept (IBC). There were hundreds of licensed advisors in attendance, and I was one of two from Canada. I didn't have the money to go, but I was determined to find answers so I wouldn't end up in the same situation as my parents. The information I learned changed my life—in large part because it was the stepping stone that led me to the book *Becoming Your Own Banker* and eventually to the man behind it all, Nelson Nash himself.

I spent the better part of a year verifying that everything I learned at this event would work in Canada. Once my business partner and I were convinced, we committed ourselves fully to implementing and teaching the process.

I'm now remarried to my beautiful wife, Rebecca. We have four children who all practice this process, along with their cousins and many other members of our extended family. We don't worry about money anymore.

My wife and I financed our first home for $426,000 in 2008 with a 40-year amortization and low interest rate. After implementing our family banking system, we paid off our home in 7 years, 33 years ahead of schedule. We did this by recapturing the debt into our own system of control exactly as we describe in this book. I know firsthand how this system can perpetuate everything in your financial world.

We have to buy things and spend money like every other family and business owner. We invest in various areas and cash-flowing assets as well. The difference? Everything— and I mean *everything*—flows through the family banking system first. We do everything that you do, but we have changed one step in the process. By implementing this change, we have drastically influenced our family's financial trajectory. Why? Because presently, $840,000 is flowing INTO our hands rather than through our hands and onto the books of someone else's bank.

To learn about Jayson's family system, access his family case study and claim your bonus content here: **DontSpreadWealth.com/bonus**

I'm not the only one with this kind of story of an upbringing spent stressed about money. In our book *Canadians*

Guide to Wealth Building Without Risk, Richard shares similar stories about his upbringing. We both know how it feels to worry constantly about money—and we both know what it feels like to be free of that worry. Just like us, you have worked hard for your money. Isn't it time for your money to work hard for you?

You've got to get into the banking business, the Family Banking Business.

A World Without Worry

Ask yourself: How would I feel if I no longer worried about money? Take a moment to imagine it. We can tell you from experience it's a peaceful, stress-free way of life.

This is a core element of how the rich get richer: putting a structure in place that alleviates worries about money. By doing this, opportunities to expand their wealth track them down because they have ready access capital to take advantage of them. My hope is that your children and my children share this message one day, coaching future generations on this process. We want to put an end to the kind of family stories that caused me so much stress.

That's why now, with 16 years of experience under our belts specializing in this process, we're showing you how to set up your family banking system and how to keep your wealth in the family—without worry.

A thinking exercise:

Add up all the money you and your family members have spent on all the things you've purchased up to this point in your lifetime.

Write the amount here (use your best guess): $_____

Could you write me a check for that amount of money right now?

The answer is NO because you did all the work to buy those things, but everyone else got all your money. That's a problem, and the Family Banking System (FBS)™ is the solution to your problem.

Your Banking Potential

Do you want some or all the money flowing back to you and your loved ones?

Here's another question: do you feel like you're not taxed enough?

No one would say they think they should be taxed more!

And who is most at risk?

YOU!

The average family in Canada pays about 43.5% of their income to both direct and indirect taxes, while the average American family pays 30%. This is summed up well in this poem:

Tax his land, tax his bed,
Tax the table at which he's fed.

Tax his work, tax his pay,
He works for peanuts anyway!

Tax his cow, tax his goat,
Tax his pants, tax his coat.

Tax his tobacco, tax his drink,
Tax him if he tries to think.

Tax his car, tax his gas,
Find other ways to tax his a$$.

Tax all he has then let him know
That you won't be done till he has no dough.

When he screams and hollers, then tax him some more,
Tax him till he's good and sore.

Then tax his coffin, tax his grave,
Tax the sod in which he's laid.

When he's gone, do not relax,
It's time to apply the inheritance tax.

These are some of the taxes you might face:

- Accounts Receivable Tax
- Airline Fuel Tax
- Airport Maintenance Tax
- Building Permit Tax
- Cigarette Tax
- Corporate Income Tax
- Death Tax
- Dog License Tax
- Driving Permit Tax
- Environmental Tax
- Excise Taxes
- Federal Income Tax
- Federal Unemployment (UI)
- Fishing License Tax
- Food License Tax
- Gasoline Tax
- Gross Receipts Tax
- Health Tax
- Hunting License Tax

- Inheritance Tax
- Interest Tax
- Liquor Tax
- Luxury Taxes
- Marriage License Tax
- Medicare Tax
- Mortgage Tax
- Personal Income Tax
- Property Tax
- Poverty Tax
- Prescription Drug Tax
- Provincial Income and Sales Tax
- Real Estate Tax
- Recreational Vehicle Tax
- Retail Sales Tax
- Service Charge Tax
- School Tax
- Telephone Federal Tax
- Telephone Federal, Provincial, and Local Surcharge Taxes
- Telephone Minimum Usage Surcharge Tax
- Vehicle License Registration Tax
- Vehicle Sales Tax
- Water Tax
- Watercraft Registration Tax
- Well Permit Tax
- Workers Compensation Tax

The more you make, the more they take. The government is constantly hovering over your family and business with a fork and knife, ready to consume your assets, income, and savings. Many would also consider inflation to be a form of hidden tax. Often this force that strips away your buying power is controlled and manipulated by a coalition of central banks and federal government policies.

Exercise:

Which of my assets are a sitting duck for future tax hikes?

List:

_____

_____

_____

_____

_____

_____

_____

_____

3

The Foundation of Sustainability

You've probably heard the phrase, "Money won't buy happiness." We believe this is true—but we also believe that bad stewardship of money will *steal* your happiness, and being poor simply won't buy you anything.

If you use money responsibly, it can be a valuable tool. If you use it carelessly, it can be a dangerous liability. When you take care of money well, you will attract more money. If you mistreat money, you will repel it. That may sound simple, but in practice, many people disrespect their money—and it all comes down to behaviors.

Building a Strong Foundation

Years ago, at an annual Conference in Birmingham, Alabama, we found ourselves standing beside the video crew at the back of the room. A presenter was on stage, pontificating about math, rates of return, and insurance product design.

Nelson Nash, who was also attending the conference, came over and tugged on Jayson's arm to get our attention. He asked us one important question:

"How long will a skyscraper stand on a weak foundation?"

When you build on a weak foundation, bad things inevitably happen. Whether through natural disasters or the simple passage of time, the structure can easily become unstable and eventually collapse, affecting many lives and often eliminating any possibility of recovery.

What Nelson was pointing out to us was that the lecturer on stage was "majoring in the minors." Nothing the lecturer was talking about mattered without a clear understanding of the process of *Becoming Your Own Banker*, The Infinite Banking Concept.

This is why it is so critical to establish a strong foundation for your Family Banking System. When you create a solid foundation, you will be able to build a system that will remain strong and last for generations to come.

Finding Your Foundation

How do you build that foundation? To start, forget that "common wisdom" we talked about in Chapter 1. If you build your foundation on myths, you will end up doing more harm than good.

Your foundation is the "why" Simon Sinek talks about in his book *Start With WHY*. You may think your financial "why" is simply to have more money but take a minute to think about it more deeply. What specifically about having more money is important to you?

Maybe you want money to take care of your family because you love them. Maybe you want to be able to live a happy life with your family, free from stress about money. If this is what you want money for, then this forms a part of your foundation. Every time you think about your finances, don't imagine a pile of money. Imagine that happy and stress-free life with your family. This image will support you and push you far more than an image of money ever will.

Maybe you don't have a family to take care of right now, but you're struggling financially in your life. If you didn't have to worry about money, what would your ideal life look like? What would you do with all the wealth you would build?

Keep digging deeper until you have a clear picture in your mind of what you want to use your money for. Really imagine it. Who is with you? What are you doing? Why is it important? How does it make you feel? Do everything you can to make it specific. The brain doesn't know how to apply its considerable resources to something that is generic. Imagine driving through dense fog on the road versus a bright, clear day of blue skies. One is far easier to see your path than the other. Set yourself up for success by framing your goals and your family with the same level of clarity.

Once you have that image in your mind, write it down. Keep it somewhere safe. That image is what you will come back to. That is the foundation of your system, and it will keep you grounded and on track, no matter what curve balls life inevitably throws your way.

In our process, we call that foundational image you wrote down your Family Banking System Statement.

Keeping Your Goal In Sight

Now that you have an outline for your foundation, you need to make sure everyone involved with your system either understands that foundation or can discern their own. If someone is going to participate in the financial value your system creates, you want them to have clarity on the foundational reasons the system is being built in the first place.

You may be successful in implementing The Infinite Banking Concept (IBC) for yourself and realizing all the benefits, but without a strong foundation, without a deep, emotional connection to *why* you are building your wealth, you and everyone around you—including the next generations—will not have the passion, the drive, to stay on target. It will be the Vanderbilt story all over again.

Without a foundation, you will end up floundering financially. Think of the lottery winners we talked about in Chapter 1: they were not thinking long-term about their money, so they ended up squandering it. They didn't have a strong foundation, so their financial building collapsed. Without a strong foundation, even great wealth has more bad consequences than benefits.

Part of building that strong foundation is talking about it. If your foundation is never a topic of conversation in your family or in your system as a whole, you set yourself up for failure, even if you were to win the lottery.

When you intentionally discuss this topic with your family, rather than waiting for a crisis to arise where you *need* to talk about it, you can more effectively plan for financial windfalls and keep that money in your family. If you don't have that foundation in place, no one will agree about how to use the money. You can pay to set up complex trusts, and you can spend hours thinking through the rules of how to implement them, but without a full-family connection to those foundational ideals, sustainability will always be at risk.

Of course, each individual in your family may picture something slightly different when they imagine what they want their money to do. But if you all communicate with each other, you can build a family foundation that incorporates everybody's vision—and you can all help keep each other on track as you build toward that future.

If your family is serious about your foundation, you can actively engage them in the process as you move through the years—and you can rest peacefully knowing they won't squander your wealth away.

Money Doesn't Ruin, It Reveals

At its core, money acts as a magnifier of one's true nature. If you're inherently kind, increased wealth often leads to even greater kindness. Conversely, if you're unkind, more money typically accentuates that trait. This concept is encapsulated in the phrase: "Money Doesn't Ruin, It Reveals."

Consider a skyscraper: with a robust foundation, it can soar skyward, embodying various elements and offering numerous possibilities, always reaching higher. However, if the foundation is frail, the entire structure risks collapsing, erasing all potential opportunities, and is fraught with danger for everyone in the vicinity of the collapse.

The pursuit of money for its own sake is a shallow endeavor. Such a mindset inevitably leads to a breaking point—either the money won't accumulate quickly enough, or the obsession with saving prevents its effective utilization. In contrast, if your financial aspirations are rooted in deeper values, like love for your family, this love becomes the driving force behind building lasting wealth. It's this foundation that not only shapes your current financial approach but also sets a precedent for future generations.

Money should amplify what you hold dear in life. If your sole focus is on wealth, your life risks becoming hollow, and your financial "house of cards" is likely to tumble. On the other hand, if your values are profound and meaningful, money can enhance these aspects, filling your life with purpose and joy.

Crafting Your Family Banking System Statement: A Quick Start Exercise

Set aside a few minutes to draft the inaugural version of your Family Banking System Statement. This statement should encapsulate your core financial priorities and serve as a source of inspiration whenever you read it. Remember, a statement that resonates with you is likely to motivate other family members as well. Aim for impact—no more than 3-5 sentences. Here's an example to guide you:

"Our family banking system unites us across generations, acting as the bond that enables a life filled with joy, purpose, giving, and productivity. By shopping at home for all the things we need and keeping the money in our family, we can achieve abundance. United, we stand resilient against economic fluctuations. Through our consistent implementation of the process of Becoming Your Own Banker, the enduring financial success and well-being of our family is assured."

Write your own below:

_____
_____
_____
_____
_____
_____
_____
_____

PART 2

The What

4

Family Financial Noise Canceling Headsets

I magine you're on a plane. In the row in front of you, a child is screaming at the top of his lungs, something about wanting another bag of pretzels. Behind you, a baby cries in response. And somehow, despite the noise, the person in the seat next to you is snoring.

And there you are, thinking, if only I had noise-canceling headphones. It's like trying to balance your checkbook in the middle of a rock concert. You're trying to talk IRAs and 401(k)s, and all you can hear is the existential scream of every dollar you've ever spent on something stupid. So, welcome to the chapter where we learn to tune out the financial equivalent of a crying baby and a snoring neighbor because, let's face it, conventional financial advice can be about as helpful as a screen door on a submarine.

Navigating through social media for insights on the "Infinite Banking Concept" (IBC) can feel like sitting in the midst of a very noisy airplane. Each post you encounter seems to contradict the previous one, creating a whirlwind of confusion. No consensus on what IBC truly is leaves you adrift in a sea of uncertainty.

Much of the online chatter zeroes in on the intricacies of a life insurance product, debating the merits of various types or designs of whole-life contracts. This conversation often falls into the trap of a one-size-fits-all mindset, ignoring the unique aspirations and requirements of individuals and families.

This issue isn't just confined to online forums; it extends to the traditional financial sector. Unfortunately, many financial professionals who attempt to adopt IBC carry over outdated practices and biases. They might lead you to believe that IBC is synonymous with a whole life insurance contract. But that's a very narrow view of a much broader concept.

IBC comprises two elements: the seen and the unseen. The policy, the tangible tool, is what you see. But the real essence of IBC lies in what you don't see, which is how the policy is utilized as a tool to implement a process. It's important to remember, as we've discussed before, that IBC has nothing to do with life insurance. It's a lifestyle of controlling how you finance the things you need in life, no longer playing Wall Street's and the bank's games and creating a peaceful, stress-free way of life financially. In fact, the principles of IBC can be applied without a dividend-paying life insurance contract. It is a process, not a product.

However, we all like efficiency, so it makes sense to use the most efficient tool at our disposal. Nelson would always say that life insurance was misclassified and, therefore fundamentally misunderstood. According to him, dividend-paying whole life insurance should be named, "a personal monetary system with a death benefit thrown in on the side for good measure."

If you want to learn more about setting a proper foundation with these insurance contracts, get yourself a copy of our second book, *Cash Follows the Leader: Uninterrupted Daily Growth with High Cash Value Insurance*. In that book, we explain the core components used to customize these unilaterally binding contracts. With this knowledge, you can be empowered to understand exactly how these contracts can be an advantage for you.

Understanding the Problem so the Solution Matters

As Nelson Nash said, "Unless you understand the problem, the solution just won't matter to you."

In the last chapter, we talked about establishing a solid foundation based on a clear and concise "why" on which to build your skyscraper. That skyscraper is your system. In order to build that skyscraper, you have to tune out all the noise.

It's not difficult to become overwhelmed by all the noise in the marketplace. Look no further than the financial news networks or publications, soundbites without substance.

Nelson Nash taught us, and we are now teaching you, that you do not need to play their game, meaning you can succeed from the banking system and become the banker as it relates to your needs. After all, the function of banking should be held at the you-and-me level. If Nelson were alive today, he would encourage you to think about that carefully because most people abdicate the responsibility, and, more importantly, the opportunity of banking in their lives. Nelson would want you to see through all the noise out there, especially as it relates to the marketing of his concept.

"Infinite Banking Concepts is ridiculously simple. It does not need to be sensationalized." - R. Nelson Nash

As market volatility continues to create uncertainty and strife, financial entertainers are coming out of the woodwork in droves, trying to claim they have the golden ticket. They tout Nelsons' concepts under some glossy label they created as the new "black box secret path" to wealth. They think they have to compete against other advisors and other policy styles or designs, so they amp up the noise in an attempt to attract your attention.

There is a reason Nelson devoted a third of his best-selling book *Becoming Your Own Banker* to describing the human conditions.

All of your money flows through someone else's bank right now—that's the problem.

What are some of life's major expenses (i.e. vehicles, homes, business equipment, appliances, holidays)?

List:

_____

_____

_____

_____

_____

_____

_____

How are these life expenses financed? Cash, leasing, loans, mortgages, and credit cards. Regardless of the method, all of these expenses are financed through someone else's banking system. You're doing all the work but someone else is getting your money.

Is that a problem? YES ___ NO: _____

If you're paying attention, you marked yes. That's why we need the Infinite Banking Concept. It is the only solution that can help you take back the money that is yours.

Nelson realized as it relates to the policy loan interest rate the life insurance company calls for, you can (and should) charge yourself more. That extra interest is not actually interest. It is simply a representation of interest and being an "honest banker." When done correctly and with good coaching, it becomes an additional premium, which adds an ever-increasing amount of accessible capital to your system. Is there any such thing as having too much capital? Have you ever read a financial news headline about a business failing because it had too much capital? Of course not. You're building a Family Banking System, and there is no such thing as too much capital in your system.

We touched on recapturing interest in Chapter 1. Now let's look at some examples to show the incredible impact this process has.

Jayson's Family Banking System

Within our banking system, we just financed a fourth vehicle. So far, on our four vehicles, we have paid $148,000 in principle and $40,675 in interest. All of those payments—principal *and* interest—have flowed back into our system of policies. We have contained the financial energy by replenishing our own money pool. Whenever we need to purchase vehicle number five, we will have access to all of the money that we repaid, plus more. Why? Because our total cash values never stop growing.

Brilliant.

Without our Family Banking System, all of that money—the $188,675—would have flowed onto the books of someone else's bank. We could never access it again, spend it again, or earn interest on it for the rest of my lifetime and every generation that comes after me. That may seem sad, yet this is how most of the car-buying public handle their affairs financially. A constant, steady stream of money away from them. How does it make you feel knowing that's what you've been doing up to this point in your lifetime? It's not your fault. The good news is that now you can change this. But there must be a *desire* to change. That's where it all begins.

When we built our new 8,000-square-foot home, we needed to purchase several new home appliances, for which we paid a total of $45,483 plus interest. Once again, that money flowed back into our Family Banking System. Education is another expense. My son attends Vimy Sports Academy, where he plays hockey. The tuition is several thousand per year. All that money flows back into our family banking system.

My $2.5 million home was also partially financed using policy loans, and yes, you guessed it, the payments flow back into our family banking system.

We created a mortgage amortization exactly the same way a regular bank would. We signed an agreement committed to sending a monthly payment, the same way a major lender would automatically withdraw a monthly payment from our account. When our private mortgage is repaid to our family banking system, we will have all the home equity, plus the equivalent of all our payments, readily accessible in our system. And we will never lose the title to our home.

Now, let's see how this all adds up:

So far, we have paid $1,000,025 plus $208,005 in interest back into our own family banking system. This number dwarfs any amount of simple interest paid to the life insurance company that we co-own. The excess interest we have committed to pay our system back over and above what the life company called for has been allocated as more premium to grow our system even further. We accomplish this by simply topping up existing policies that have room for the funds or by adding new life insurance policies on someone we have a beneficial interest in (i.e. another family member, a business partner, etc.). Quite simply, we do exactly what our mentor, Nelson Nash, taught us to do, and it has completely liberated us financially.

If we did not have our Family Banking System in place, we would still need money, and we would have to purchase all those things I shared with you. The difference is that without the system, I would've done all the work, and everyone else would have gotten all the money. I would have achieved the objective of purchasing all of those goods and services, but I could no longer use that money. I would continue making a good living, but the banks would make an even better living off me.

We've put a stop to that, and so can you.

This is only a small sample size of the impact this system has on my family's wealth. I am also privileged to be the chairman of the Lowe Family Group of Companies. We started our first company in a basement, and we now have twelve different operating companies, which combined produce eight figures a year in gross revenue!

And just like commercial banks, we are keeping that revenue in constant motion. The money flows back to our system of policies rather than away from our companies.

We were only able to build this because I had ready access to capital with which I could take advantage of high-caliber opportunities. We have been truly blessed—and we owe it all to the process we are sharing with you here.

"When you have ready-access capital, opportunities of
high caliber will track you down."
—R. Nelson Nash

Navigating the Maze: Choose Wisdom Over Greed

Expanding your wealth is achievable, but it requires knowledge about where to start and whom to trust. The most effective wealth-building strategies often diverge from the mainstream path. Quick-fix solutions touted by many aren't always swift or dependable. True wealth growth necessitates patience and a long-range perspective.

Savvy investors, for example, understand the risks of blindly following popular investment trends. A stock's over-investment inflates its price, making such trendy options a potential path to overpayment. Hence, when the crowd is greedy, be cautious.

The rush towards fast money schemes is akin to entering a burning building. Instead of joining the crowd rushing in, be the one who wisely chooses to exit. People may advise investing in mutual funds and registered accounts like 401Ks and RRSPs. But here's an insight: in all our experience, we've never met someone who amassed significant wealth through either of these channels. This observation delivers a clear message: the path to substantial wealth isn't through mutual funds or 401Ks. To elevate your financial status, consider whether to follow the masses or the methods of the actual wealthy.

Success leaves clues. Emulate what the wealthy do, not what financial gurus on social media suggest. The key is to maintain control over your finances. Conforming to popular opinion won't yield the desired results. Dare to be different, make informed decisions, and adopt a system that aligns with your goals. This approach is a sustainable and secure method to grow your wealth, and it's precisely what a family banking system offers.

Seize Opportunity: Your Path to Wealth

Cultivating your family banking system begins with desire and demands dedication, courageous actions, and rethinking your thinking. It involves defining clear objectives for yourself and your family.

The path to real wealth accumulation and preservation among the affluent doesn't lie in mimicking the average person. They avoid wasteful and impulsive spending. Instead, they reinvest their resources into self-growth and pursuits that amplify their wealth, unafraid to forge their own unique path.

Consider the story of Andrew Carnegie, a quintessential rags-to-riches narrative. Carnegie's humble beginnings in a one-room house in Scotland didn't define his future. After moving to the United States, he started working in a textile mill, climbed the ranks, and eventually led the western division of the Pennsylvania Railroad.

Carnegie didn't squander his earnings or conform to the financial habits of his peers. He steered clear of trendy investments that could lead to losses. With his earnings, he founded the Carnegie Steel Company, building it into an industrial titan. His success stemmed not from following others but from paving his own way, rail by rail.

Carnegie's tale of diligence and success isn't an isolated incident. With the process we provide, you, too, can construct your journey, laying each rail towards the life you desire. This context means understanding what's best for you and your family and pursuing it, even if it contradicts popular opinion.

"Everything that you do financially is compared to what
everyone else is doing financially"
—R. Nelson Nash

It's also about skillfully managing your wealth to ensure
its growth. This means making smart financial choices, not
resorting to short-sighted measures. Embrace the mindset of
seizing opportunities and make decisions that lead to lasting
prosperity.

5

The Family Grocery Business

Revisiting an earlier thought process: If you co-owned a Safeway grocery store, would you ever buy your food from Walmart? Of course not! Why would you spend your money with a competitor when you could be spending it at your own business? By that same token, if you have your own family banking system, you don't want to finance life's purchases through someone else's bank.

If you did, all of that financial energy leaves your system, never to return. When you "shop at home" by accessing policy loans from your family banking system and repaying them responsibly, all of that financial energy (the money) flows back into your system and can be reutilized. And, because we're utilizing dividend-paying life insurance contracts as the tool to implement the process, there are tax-free windfalls of death benefit proceeds that will replenish and expand the family's money pool.

You are going to die someday.

Having policies in place means that financial security is assured because all the money spent is replenished and then transferred to the next generation on a tax-free basis. It's brilliant.

Every decision you make with money is a financing decision. There are no exceptions. If you are paying interest to someone else—shopping at someone else's grocery store—you are permanently giving away money that you could have earned for yourself. Money you spend that could have been used for something else is called your "opportunity cost."

Here's an example of what opportunity cost means: you paid $30,000 cash for your car; now you cannot use that $30,000 or earn interest on it ever again. The opportunity cost is all the lost interest earnings over your lifetime and every generation that comes after you. It should be no surprise why banks make so much money for their stockholders. They've done a very convincing job of compelling you to continue transferring your money to them so they can keep it in constant motion, never foregoing the opportunity to earn more interest.

Here are some other opportunity cost examples:

Example	Earning potential	Time Period	Foregone Interest Earnings
$25,000 for one year of university	4%	30 years	$57,837.45
$30,000 for a wedding	4%	30 years	$69,404.94
$20,000 for a used car	4%	30 years	$46,269.96
$200,000 for a down payment on a property	4%	30 years	$462,699.60

Over this time frame of 30 years, this represents 3.24 times more capital if the original value was left to grow at a simple, basic savings rate. If you are 40 years old, that would be retirement cash available at age 70. If you are 60 years old, this represents estate value that would never pass on to your loved ones.

But what if you could recapture the foregone interest earnings? You can, if you have your own banking system. By running these purchases through your own system, you become all four characters in the financial play (the depositor, borrower, banker, and bank owner). Many people understand the concept of lost opportunity cost, but very few actually reckon with it because they don't know how. And so all that money keeps flowing away from them. Now, you can stop your money from flowing away from you and recapture that lost opportunity cost.

Don't Steal the Peas

Imagine you're the proud owner of that Safeway grocery store. Picture the aisles: are they well stocked and faced with a variety of products your customers desire, or are they barren? Just as a successful grocery store continuously restocks its shelves to satisfy customer needs, your family banking system needs a steady flow of stock—and in this case, that stock is money.

Consider this: when your fridge or pantry runs out of groceries, you replenish them. Similarly, your financial "shelves" need regular restocking. Continuously withdrawing from your financial reserves without replenishing them is like letting your grocery store's shelves go empty, leaving your family's needs unmet. Remember, your family always requires food, just as you always need money.

You wouldn't sneak peas from your store's shelves and walk out the back door without paying, right? That would be stealing your own inventory. Similarly, if you take policy loans and fail to repay them, anyone involved in your family banking system will only see scarcity, not prosperity. Not repaying loans is like removing goods from your grocery store shelves without restocking them.

If your family consistently depletes the money from your system without replenishing it, profit remains elusive. And like a grocery store with empty shelves is unappealing to customers, a depleted banking system is unattractive to your family. Continual depletion without profit leads to financial disaster.

Therefore, it's crucial to repay your policy loans with additional interest (remember, that extra interest is more premium to expand your system). Neglecting this not only prevents your "store" from making a profit but also hinders the growth of your family's wealth. Merely returning what you borrowed keeps you at a standstill, not moving forward. To truly nourish your family's banking system, you need to do more than that; you need to grow your money pool. This approach is fundamental to building and sustaining wealth.

Expand Your Store

Would you have much of a grocery store business if you were the only customer who shopped there? Of course not! You need to make sure that not only your needs are met, but the needs of your customers as well. Keeping your store stocked can feed your family and everyone within your system. When we invite new family members into our system, we want to make sure it is stocked with money.

We know it can be nerve-wracking to involve others in this kind of big, bold financial move—but your family needs to eat, too. Why not invite them to be customers of your grocery store?

You can start by focusing on your immediate family, working with one of our coaches to properly implement steps to build and utilize your banking system. Once your immediate family has a solid handle on the process, you can then involve your extended family and even start the process with business partners.

Engaging the Whole Family: Financial Wisdom for All Ages

Incorporating your family into your banking system isn't just about involving the adults; it's crucial to include the kids too! Much like young children pick up new languages more easily, introducing them to the concept of family banking early on sets a strong foundation. Before they're exposed to the complex world of finance, children can grasp the basics of the family's financial strategy with surprising ease.

Now, let's be realistic: kids aren't going to be enthralled by discussions of interest rates or the intricacies of dividend-paying life insurance policies. What they do understand, however, is the simple concept of a cash register. They know that if you own it and you take money out, you need to put it back. And if you return it with a little extra, the cash register grows fuller! This straightforward analogy can make explaining the system to young ones both fun and effective.

By consistently "paying it forward" within this system, you're setting up a self-sustaining financial model—think of it as a perpetual grocery store that can support and enrich your family for generations to come. This approach not only simplifies financial education for kids but also instills valuable lessons about responsibility and growth from a young age.

One of the resources we have put together for you as part of our bonuses is an incredible discussion with Jayson's children you can use as inspiration. They share their experience of implementing this incredible life-changing process at a young age. You can watch an interview with Jayson's ten-year-old daughter, his 14-year-old son, and his 14-year-old nephew in front of 200 attendees in Toronto, Canada. Access all of your book bonuses here: **DontSpreadWealth.com/bonus**

Leading by Example

We already talked about the dangers of stealing the peas from your grocery store. What lesson does that teach your children, their friends, or extended family who also rely on your store? Remember, you're the role model—what you do sets the standard for everyone else. It's a classic case of "monkey see, monkey do." Disrespect your family banking system, and others will follow suit. Ignore the rules and watch as others do the same.

Your responsibility extends beyond mere rule-setting; it's about embodying respect for your family's banking system. If not, the entire framework could collapse. Consider the future: when you're gone, and your children inherit a significant amount of tax-free death benefit proceeds, the wealth you've diligently built, what then? Without proper guidance and a clear example to emulate, they might succumb to the overwhelming financial "noise." Lacking essential skills and understanding, they might drift towards other "stores" (i.e. someone else's bank), squandering the wealth you've all worked so hard to accumulate.

Building and maintaining wealth is a constant challenge without a robust system. And a vital component of this system is ensuring everyone comprehends and respects it. Failure to instill this understanding risks the collapse of everything you've built.

However, if you exemplify good stewardship, you can inspire the same in your successors. You have the power to influence them to continue nurturing and expanding the family business. Children absorb the lessons they're taught, both good and bad. Seize this opportunity to steer the ship, guiding your family through calm and stormy seas alike. This isn't only about managing a system; it's about instilling a legacy of wisdom and responsibility that endures through generations.

Let's look at some real-life examples. These are some people who have faced the bitter reality of financial troubles, and by embracing the system, they were able to pull themselves out.

Allan and Janet Antonio are real estate investors in their 50s. Before the Family Banking System, they were unsuccessful with investing. They lost a lot of money in a tax-qualified plan (RRSP) and turned to real estate, wanting to make the wheels of the banking business and real estate turn. A year after they purchased their first policy, they purchased five more policies. They expanded their program to include all their grandchildren. Within three years, they eliminated three mortgages and were 13 years ahead of schedule. They were even able to finance their daughter's first home from their family bank.

Now, their college funds for their grandchildren and their passive income in retirement are both assured. They have been able to create generational wealth for their children and grandchildren. As of today, they have $4.1 million total permanent death benefit, rising annually. When death comes, and it will come, the family will receive death benefit proceeds, income tax free, and the family's money pool will be replenished again with everything the life insured spent plus more.

They say, "The Family Banking System Jayson and his teammates have taught us is providing financial security and certainty for all of us in our family. It is definitely a win, win, win."

Another man, Jim, paid $595,000 in premiums by the age of 65. His Family Banking System accessed $1,785,000 to finance whatever they needed. By age 90, his net death benefit was $2,714,495, refilling his family money pool with the $2,380,000 ($595K + $1.785 million) plus $334,495 in additional windfall . . . ALL tax-free.

Another example. Martin and Bonnie Dansereau are in their 50s and own a vacuum truck business. They established a profitable business, saving money in a sinking fund in someone else's bank to purchase trucks and cover maintenance. This approach permanently transferred money away from them, and they got caught in a cycle of investing, saving, and spending with all their money residing in someone else's system.

When they started implementing the Family Banking System, they had a $50,000 annual premium and expanded by an additional $50,000 per year. Their starting death benefit was $1.8 million. Four years in, they self financed a $400,000 vacuum truck utilizing policy loans. They control the repayment schedule and recapture all the money. Their death benefit is $6.4 million and rising.

Their cash value (which is not money) continues piling up daily, and it cannot go backward. It is contractually guaranteed to match their total death benefit (which also increases every year) by age 100 of each life that is insured.

These people prove that when you follow this process, your financial goals become achievable realities. They are leaving lasting legacies for their families for generations to come. They have started their own grocery store, and they're not stealing the peas!

6

Planning for Windfalls

At the beginning of *The Lion King*, life is going great for young Simba. He's looking forward to becoming king, and in the meantime, he's enjoying life with his best friend, doing whatever he wants, whenever he wants.

Suddenly, everything changes. His father dies. His own life at risk, he runs away from home and stumbles upon a new life where nothing is familiar.

Life is never going to be all sunshine and rainbows. There are inevitably going to be downs to go with the ups. Maybe there will even be dramatic events that change your whole life, just like Simba.

The one certainty in life is that nothing is certain. Things aren't always going to go as you expect (with the exception of cash values in life insurance, which always go up). But there is one thing you can do: prepare as best you can.

Nelson Nash taught us to think 70 years down the line. It is very likely that we won't be here, but our future generations will. The reality is most of us can't plan past this weekend. By changing the way we think and preparing for a bigger future now, we can help ourselves and our descendants.

Always be thinking three generations
past your own.

If a disaster occurs, your finances often take a big hit. You have no way of knowing if or when such a thing might happen. You might think you have plenty of time to build a safety net, but there's no telling what might happen. It's best to start building that net now. Because while you might not have the weight of a future kingdom on your shoulders, you do have a family to provide for.

Disasters happen without warning all the time, and if you aren't prepared, you might feel the urge to flee, just like Simba. But when something bad happens, it doesn't have to mean financial disaster. With proper planning and a good system in place, you can survive the turmoil with your finances intact.

Here's an example:

Say a family spends three million dollars over the course of 30 years—at which point the patriarch of the family dies. Normally, we might expect only problems to be left behind in this situation. But this family created a system whereby all the money they spent was being replenished throughout their lifetimes. When the patriarch dies, their tax-free death benefit goes back into the system.

Thanks to this, the family is able to take the time they need to grieve properly without a financial mess hanging over their heads they have to worry about dealing with. People never pass away at the "right time," but by creating a solid system, you'll see that you can take care of as much of the financial planning as possible so you can be prepared when it does happen.

We know because we've experienced this ourselves.

Jayson's Story

My father-in-law retired from police service after a multi-decade career. Soon after his retirement, we introduced him to the Infinite Banking Concept. My father-in-law swore he wasn't insurable because of his type two diabetes, but we got him approved. Never assume you aren't insurable—it's always worth trying to insure yourself. You are risking so much if you don't.

We purchased two policies for my father-in-law, promising that I would pay the premiums and assuring my mother-in-law (Nonna) that if my father-in-law passed first, she would never have a bad financial day for the rest of her lifetime. We also promised to put policies in place on all nine of his grandkids as his legacy to them.

We could easily have put off doing this. We believed he was going to live a long time. It would have been easy to say, "We'll do this later." Thankfully, we didn't wait—and in 2017, we purchased both policies. Very sadly, Papa was diagnosed with cancer in 2020, and five weeks later, he passed away.

This tragedy hit our family out of nowhere and was over heartbreakingly quickly. If we hadn't preemptively made a plan, he never would have been able to pass this legacy down to his grandchildren. Because we did make this plan and fulfilled our promises, his impact will continue, and he will live on in our family.

The year before my father-in-law passed, the family was all together on vacation in California, and all the kids were coming up to me at the restaurant dinner table, giving me kisses just like my daughters always do. My father-in-law, watching this, leaned into me and said, "You see all these kids? They love you. You're the godfather of this whole family—and now, they are your responsibility."

I will never forget this. It's exactly why I fight for the banking system in our family. He charged me with protecting my family, and that is what I will do—and, thanks to Nelson's mentorship and what he pioneered with IBC, will continue to do even after I am gone.

The Family Banking System is not only about all the living benefits and financing control. There are also death benefits for all the lives insured in the family. Many people who learn about this concept will downplay the value or importance of the tax-free death benefit. Never underestimate the power of this precious resource. Nobody has a lease on life. And so, while we do not know when we will pass, we do know that when we see the hearse driving on the roadway, they're not practicing.

My late mentor Bob Shiels often said, "I wish that everyone could die once, just for a week, and see the problems they leave behind."

The Family Banking System solves those problems because a windfall of tax-free money shows up exactly when it's needed the most. Every day that you delay is another day you penalize yourself and your family.

Taking care of your family doesn't have to be complicated. The sooner you start, the better prepared you can be for any future tragedies or windfalls that might hit your family.

The Power of Live Steam

Of course, life doesn't only hold tragedies—it also holds triumphs. I, Jayson, will share another example:

Years ago, I looked into taking out a policy that had a $20,000 annual premium, and the minimum base premium was $15,000. That was a lot of money for me at the time. I instantly got nervous about fitting it into my budget.

I asked Nelson for advice. "All right," he said, "work with what you've got."

And that's what I did.

Think about a tree stump.

Each ring represents one year of the tree's uninterrupted growth. Each year, another ring is added—but rings are never taken away. The stump never shrinks. It is impossible to go back in time and take away years of that tree's life. For as long as the tree is alive, Mother Nature constantly supplies it with water and nutrients so it can keep growing.

The same is true of your dividend paying life insurance contract. Once I decided to go ahead with this policy, I started building a system that could only expand.

In 2013, we received our first dividend. I took the whole family on vacation, and in 2014, we recaptured all of that money. In 2015, we purchased a Honda Odyssey—and recaptured all of that money. In 2016, we received our fourth dividend. In 2017, we bought our second car—and recaptured all of that money. In 2018 and 2019, we went on more family vacations.

You can see how it all starts to add up when you take the financial energy away from outside lenders and redirect it into your own system. And the more you do it, the more capacity you create.

If you take a pail of water and heat it to 210 degrees Fahrenheit, all you have is very hot water. But if you heat it just 2 degrees more, you get something else: steam with unbelievable power. This power only comes out when you get past the boiling point—and you need a lot of energy to get to that point. If you remove the pail at 210 degrees, all you have is really hot water . . . all the energy that was used to get it there begins to dissipate, and you will never see the results of the effort you put into heat it. But, if you wait till the boiling point, the result is immense. After all, the steam-powered engine changed the world!

In October 2012, the premium I paid for this one policy was a total of $20,000. In October 2023, the grand total of premiums I paid was $240,000. The total cash value in our first year was $4,500. As of May 20, 2024, it is $264,387.59 —and it keeps increasing every day.

Between 2012 and 2024, we raised the heat until we got full steam power by continuing to pay a premium into our system.

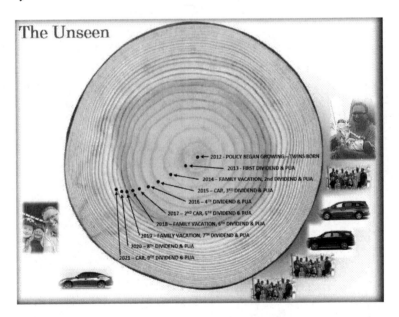

The Unseen

2012 - POLICY BEGAN GROWING - TWINS BORN
2013 - FIRST DIVIDEND & PUA
2014 - FAMILY VACATION, 2nd DIVIDEND & PUA
2015 - CAR, 3RD DIVIDEND & PUA
2016 - 4TH DIVIDEND & PUA
2017 - 2ND CAR, 5TH DIVIDEND & PUA
2018 - FAMILY VACATION, 6TH DIVIDEND & PUA
2019 - FAMILY VACATION, 7TH DIVIDEND & PUA
2020 - 8TH DIVIDEND & PUA
2021 - CAR, 9TH DIVIDEND & PUA

You can watch a deep dive review of this policy snapshot over a 10-year period and see exactly how we achieved the power of live "financial steam" here: **DontSpreadWealth.com/bonus**

People often ask, "How soon can I stop paying the premium for this policy?" But that's not the question you should be asking. Instead, ask: "Why would I ever stop depositing the premium for this policy?"

In 2023, I paid another $20,000 in annual premiums. The dividend paid was $9,190.45, and the cash value increased $30,000 from 2022 to 2023. How's that for beating the pants off inflation?

Knowing that it keeps getting more efficient, when would I ever stop paying $20,000 in premium into a policy that grows more than $30,000 in cash value over a 12-month window?

NEVER.

If you ask yourself the same question, I suspect you will arrive at the same conclusion. With that in mind you can start to see both how and why my family system has grown based on the following chart.

As at May 20, 2024, here's a snapshot of our Lowe Family Banking System, which includes business partners and key employees in our family group of companies.

Lowe Family Banking System	2009	2024	
Number of Policies	2	77	*27 Lives Insured
Total Annual Premium	$16,800	$1,050,000	
Total Death Benefit	$500,000	$40,801,969	*continually rising
Total Cash Value	$4,250	$3,799,438	*rising daily
Loans	$300	$1,656,438	*unstructured
Loan Amount Available	$3,825	$1,763,056	*rising daily
Loan Repayments back to our Family	$330	$70,000 per month ($840,000 / YR)	
Windfalls	$0	2 death benefit proceeds	

We no longer rely upon a conventional bank for anything other than the convenience of a debit card! $70,000 every month flows back to my family's money pool. That's $840,000 a year.

Imagine having additional money flowing back into your family's money pool.

How much more could you achieve in your savings and lifestyle?

Answer:

_____

_____

_____

_____

If you worked for a commercial bank, would you want customers to stop depositing their money with your bank? I think not!

Your money has to reside somewhere, and there's no better place for it to reside than in your own family banking system. As you practice this concept it becomes natural to grow your system. If you are consistently maxing out your premiums each year, you can simply purchase additional policies to expand your system. This can be another policy on yourself, another on a family member, or perhaps a joint venture or business partner. It could be a conversion of strategically placed term insurance that has been set up in mind for your future expansion. With the number of policies we have in our system, if the policy that we access the loan from cannot hold the extra premium, the extra premium goes into a policy that will hold it. If there is no room, then we strategize on what the next policy should be, including who it should be on.

Our Two Rules

Just as a commercial bank needs many depositors, your banking system ultimately needs more than your immediate family. Luckily, there are many reasons your extended family may want to be invited into your system. Maybe they need money for a vehicle or a house. Maybe they want to consolidate debt.

With a family banking system, you can say, "Come see me, and I'll take care of it for you." But when you do this, there are two conditions you must have—the same conditions we always use for our family banking systems.

First, they have to repay the loans at your interest rate, no exceptions. The schedule for repayment is negotiable, but the interest rate is not. Second, you have to be able to coach them on how to do it. As we've mentioned before, the system will fail if you're not creating generational knowledge by passing on the knowledge we are teaching you.

And that's it! Once people see the way the family banking system can benefit them and their loved ones, they'll want in—and there's very little required of them to do so. Keep your system stocked, and people will come.

But the investment doesn't stop there. Once you get people on board, it's important to check in with them about what's going on in the system. How do you do this? By holding a periodic Family Banking Meeting. We recommend at least annually but many will choose to do it even more frequently.

PART 3

The How

7

How to Conduct Your Family Banking Meeting

What do you think of when you hear the word "meeting"? Is it a room with a long table and people wearing suits? Is it a boring slideshow that you know could have been an email?

That's not what your family banking meeting should be. You don't want it to be a tedious task people do only out of obligation. It should be a meaningful time for asking questions and discussing what is important to your family.

Have you ever had a boss who never communicated his plans with the team, who expects you to know what he's thinking without him saying it? They're often the same bosses who shut down questions and don't allow you to openly share feedback. All you can do is stick to your own work and try to predict what your boss will do next. You always feel like you're playing catch-up as new projects and rules are thrown at you unexpectedly.

This is what your family banking system would be like without meetings: no open space for people to ask questions or talk about what is or isn't working, no awareness of what is happening in the system, and no opportunity to offer encouragement. Without that, your family will likely leave the system, and the ones who stay will not be getting as much out of it as they could.

Who's At the Meeting?

Before you can have a meeting, you need to know who wants to be part of the system.

Don't be discouraged if a family member chooses not to participate. This system cannot be forced on someone, and you cannot teach it through argument. We know how frustrating it can be—feeling like you have the solution to all your family's money problems, but they just won't listen. Perhaps they don't quite understand the benefits, or perhaps there's something else going on you don't know about. You can try to convince them, but if they aren't budging, it's not worth arguing—no matter how disheartening it is.

When we've been frustrated about someone not joining our systems, we ask ourselves, "What would I be doing right now if I wasn't bothered by this?" If the answer is "hanging out with my kids"—we go hang out with our kids. If the answer is "read a book"—we go read a book. We excuse ourselves from the conversation, wish them a good rest of the day, and leave it at that.

The best way to convince a family member to join your system is to keep building it and show them how well it works. They might come around just by seeing your example! This has been our experience and slowly but surely has allowed us to expand our meetings, our system, and our impact.

Conducting a Meeting

Once you know who is on board with the system, you can select a date for the family banking meeting. It's important to be clear about expectations for this meeting—such as that everyone will attend the meeting, including children. Children actually often understand the system more quickly than adults, and they can unexpectedly offer incredibly insightful comments! You can hear an interview with two of Jayson's children discussing their thoughts on the family banking system here: **DontSpreadWealth.com/bonus**

Once you have everyone assembled, here are some of the "Dos" for running your meeting:

- Choose a family-appointed representative to chair it.

- Always take notes and record the meeting.

- Be intentional about recognizing what is going well. If someone has recently accessed or repaid a loan, applaud them. If someone has insured a new family member, recognize them. Celebrate people when they are doing things right, and you will encourage them and others to keep up the good work.

- Review any updates to your system.

- Have a Q&A time, where anyone can ask any questions they have and better understand any challenging parts. This needs to be a time where people feel comfortable, where they can talk about what interests them and what they're confused about. In your meetings, one person should never be doing all the talking.

- Always follow up with family members, especially if they want to talk about something in private.

You can download a family banking workbook with a template agenda of a family banking meeting here: **DontSpreadWealth.com/bonus**

One additional thing we have found very impactful in our meetings is to read sections of Nelson's book. We'll pick up the book and flip until someone says stop, then we'll dive into that portion and discuss it. That becomes your coaching topic for the meeting. You can use it to teach the ideas of the system and expand on what you already know. Share your thoughts with each other, ask questions, go deeper than the surface of the main ideas.

You want your family to know what you've created, and you want them to create it for themselves, too. Out of this discussion, you can talk about important topics like estate planning, review of wills, power of attorney, and personal directives.

You could also watch the Nelson Nash documentary. We actually require people who are new to our system to read Nelson's book and watch the documentary. Simply hearing about this concept once will not fully instill it. The more you study it and talk about it, the more you remind yourself of the value of the concept, the sharper your knowledge and understanding will become, and the more you can improve your own system.

We also like to talk about Nelson Nash's influence as a whole. We want our family members to remember who this system came from. To our kids, Nelson has become a storybook character, like Santa. That's how they can best understand him and his influence on our lives. We always want to remember and venerate the person who mentored us and taught us about this life-changing system.

We have a huge amount of content available for you and your family to really study and understand this concept: **DontSpreadWealth.com/bonus**

Through these meetings, you will instill the fundamental truths we've been discussing: knowing who controls the banking function of your life, remembering that your money must reside somewhere, so it's best to have it reside with you, and understanding that you don't have to be rich to build and utilize this system. The knowledge and good money habits you instill in your children will continue through the generations as your children pass them on to their children.

Through these meetings, you can create a cycle of wealth and knowledge instead of poverty and ignorance.

You Will Never Be Younger Than Right Now

What is the best time to start these meetings? The answer is easy: Right. Now.

Imagine your future. Maybe you want to get married or have a child. Maybe you want that promotion at work or are looking forward to retirement and spending time with your grandkids. No matter what you want your future to look like, there is one future certainty we all have in common: we will get older.

Whoever you are thinking about insuring, we encourage you to do it without delay—even your kids and grandkids. In Canada and the United States, you can insure a newborn as early as 16 *days* old. Imagine how much bigger your system would be if you insured someone at 16 days instead of 16 years!

We've included an example of Richard showing his own children's policies and what they can accomplish over a lifespan. You can access this case study here: **DontSpreadWealth.com/bonus**

Once those contracts are in place, they can never be taken away. You will always be in complete control of them, and they will continue to expand from the moment you set them up. If you restrict your system to your immediate family, you prevent it from growing, and you prevent others from getting those benefits. Share the good news with your family and friends. Gather them into the fold. The only thing preventing your system from growing today is you.

No matter how many people you have in your system, it will never be fully healthy if you are not all meeting together to discuss it. In order to maintain a well-maintained system, it is vital for everyone to stay informed. If you follow our structure, you will see how healthy your system can become.

8

Dispelling Misleading Statements and Half-Truths about the Infinite Banking Concept

I n the world of finance, misinformation, and half-truths can easily derail even the most well-intentioned plans. IBC is no exception. This chapter aims to clear up common misconceptions and provide a clearer understanding of what IBC truly involves. Let's address some prevalent myths and misleading statements head-on.

1. You Can Buy an "Infinite Banking Policy"

The Truth: There is No Such Thing

You cannot buy an "Infinite Banking Policy" because it doesn't exist. What you are purchasing is dividend-paying whole life insurance contracts. The Infinite Banking Concept is a process you implement using these contracts as the best tool to get the job done. It's crucial to distinguish between what you're buying (the insurance contracts) and what you're implementing (the Infinite Banking Concept). This distinction helps clarify that IBC is a process, not a product.

2. One Dollar Doing the Job of Two Dollars

The Truth: This is Simply Misleading

Many claim that you can have one dollar doing the job of two dollars, but this is misleading. The cash value in your policy is not actual money; it represents the net present value of the future payment of a death benefit. When you access a policy loan, you are not doubling your money. Your premiums and loan repayments are dollars you pay into the life insurance company. The dollars you borrow are the life insurance company's money, which you then use to control how you finance your needs. Understanding this distinction helps set realistic expectations about the characteristics of your policy or system of policies.

3. Think About Premiums as Deposits

The Truth: Premiums Are Payments, Not Deposits

Another common misconception is thinking of premiums as deposits. This is incorrect. A premium has always been and always will be a payment. When you pay your premium, you are making a payment to the insurance company for the benefits and coverage provided by your policy. It's essential to recognize this to avoid confusion and to appreciate the nature of your financial commitments within the IBC framework.

4. Save Earning 4%, Borrow at 6%, and Come Out Ahead

The Truth: This is Misleading

Saying you can earn 4%, borrow at 6%, and come out ahead is misleading because it oversimplifies the complex interplay of interest rates, compounding effects, and the time value of money. Over the long term, borrowing at a higher rate than your savings rate leads to financial loss, not gain. This scenario oversimplifies the complexities of interest rates and financial growth. Realistically, the goal of IBC is to control how you finance your purchases and recapture the interest you would otherwise pay to external lenders, not to play a numbers game with interest rates.

5. Get Rich Buying <INSERT PRODUCT HERE>

The Truth: IBC is About Controlling HOW you Finance the Things You Need

The Infinite Banking Concept is not about getting rich by buying specific products. It's about how you control the financing of the things you need throughout your lifetime. The primary goal is to recapture the interest you're currently paying to banks, credit card companies, and finance companies and redirect that financial energy back into your own system. This approach helps you build a peaceful, stress-free way of life financially.

6. There is Only One Way to Design a Policy to Implement IBC

The Truth: This is Absurd

The statement that there is only one correct way to design a policy and that any other way means the advisor only cares about commissions is absurd. Life insurance companies set their own commission schedules, and if you are getting the value you expect, the advisor's commission should not be your concern. When you shop for groceries, you don't ask how much the store employees are paid; you focus on the convenience, product availability, and service. Similarly, the design of your policy should be based on your needs and objectives and the ongoing coaching and service you should expect, not on the advisor's compensation.

7. Paying Yourself More Interest Grows Your Wealth

The Truth: More Interest is More Premium

The idea that paying yourself more interest than the insurance company requires will grow your wealth is not accurate. The extra interest you pay is not really interest; it's more premium. The only thing that truly grows your system is more premium. This means that the growth of your wealth within the IBC framework is directly tied to the amount of premium you contribute to your policies and for how long.

Conclusion

Clearing up these common misconceptions is crucial for anyone considering the Infinite Banking Concept. By understanding the truth behind these statements, you can better appreciate the value of IBC and implement it more effectively in your lifestyle. Remember, IBC is about adopting a process to control HOW you finance the things you need throughout your lifetime.

Implementing the Infinite Banking Concept is best accomplished with the support of an experienced coach, and working with a knowledgeable coach can make all the difference. At Ascendant Financial in Canada and LifEVA in the United States, we are dedicated to helping you navigate this process. As of 2024, we are entering our 16th year of serving people just like you, and we would love to share a personalized conversation with you.

Partnering with us means gaining access to all our extensive experience, resources, and personalized guidance tailored to your unique financial situation. We are committed to your success and passionate about helping you achieve financial independence and security through the Infinite Banking Concept. Don't let misconceptions hold you back—reach out to Ascendant Financial or LifEVA today, and let's make your financial objectives achievable realities.

9

Take Control Back

No one walks the path of life alone. We all need good people around us to lift us up, inspire us, and make the journey worthwhile. Your family is an integral part of this ongoing process, and your futures are linked together in many ways. Financially, our lives are connected through pivotal events that impact multiple family members, such as the birth of a child, college education, weddings, buying a home, family vacations, health issues, or the passing of a family member.

These events highlight the significant role of money in our lives, and the impact can be either positive or negative. For instance, a family vacation can create powerful memories but also be a financial drain impacting future retirement. Implementing the Family Banking System can forever improve these pivotal moments.

Imagine containing all the financial energy within a holding tank that allows everyone to prosper perpetually. This approach provides more peace of mind and financial stability. According to the Washington Post, it costs $310,000 USD to raise a child to age 18. Considering modern inflation and extended dependency periods, these costs will only increase. With the Family Banking System, you can manage the financial responsibilities of raising a child and other significant life expenses more effectively.

Reclaiming Financial Control

Reclaiming control of your finances through the Family Banking System involves the following key steps:

1. **Building a Pool of Capital:** Intentionally build a pool of capital within an entity that guarantees daily growth of cash value and provides ready access to money on demand, on your terms.

2. **Recapturing Interest:** Recapture the interest and money you pay to banks now and in the future by using your pool of capital to finance all your needs throughout your lifetime.

3. **Protecting Wealth:** Safeguard your livelihood, real estate portfolios, investments, and retirement accounts from being decimated by high levels of taxation.

By implementing the Family Banking System, you shift from being controlled by debt and external financial institutions to calling the shots financially. This empowerment leads to financial independence, economic security, and the creation of wealth that aligns with your personal values and goals.

Advantages of Taking Control Back

1. **Economic Independence:** You gain control over your economic future, reducing reliance on commercial banks and external financial systems.

2. **Wealth Creation:** By keeping the financial energy within your family, you ensure continual growth of your wealth and protection from market volatility and taxation.

3. **Generational Impact:** The system allows you to build a legacy of financial wisdom and security, ensuring that future generations benefit from your foresight and planning.

4. **Access to Opportunities:** Having ready access to capital on your terms allows you to seize high-caliber investment opportunities, further enhancing your wealth.

Practical Implementation

Start small by involving your immediate family in the system, gradually expanding to include extended family members. Regular family banking meetings help everyone stay informed, involved, and aligned with the system's goals. This collaborative approach not only builds financial stability but also strengthens family bonds.

In conclusion, the Family Banking System is not just a financial strategy; it's a movement towards reclaiming control over your financial life. By embracing this system, you break free from the cycle of debt and financial insecurity, creating a future where your family's wealth is preserved and passed down through generations.

Your Invitation to Financial Freedom: Begin Your Journey Now!

Congratulations on reaching this pivotal moment in our book! Your continued reading signals a readiness for change—a desire to break free from traditional banking and take control of your financial destiny. You're not just seeking knowledge; you're ready for action. And the good news? You don't need to be rich to get into the family banking business. We're here to guide you every step of the way.

The journey begins with one simple yet transformative step: establishing your family banking system. You know you deserve this change, and deep down, you believe your family does too. And let us assure you, this isn't just theory; it's a proven path to financial independence.

Consider Jayson's daughter, Katelynn, already holding six policies and a growing pool of cash value at 10 years old. She's set for life, free from the need for commercial banks. Or Jayson's nephew Ethan, a budding entrepreneur at 16, who's already using his financial knowledge to profit and reinvest. And Jayson's son, Jackson, has been actively managing and repaying policy loans since he was 11. Even Jayson's twin daughters are deeply involved in annual banking meetings, absorbing invaluable financial lessons. Their success will not be from the policies themselves but from the mindset and training they have been receiving as part of ongoing family gatherings and constant involvement in the family banking system.

More powerful than fiction, these stories are real-life examples of financial empowerment. Imagine a life where credit applications, dependence on commercial banks, and financial worries are things of the past. This can be your reality, regardless of your age or current financial status. The

Infinite Banking Concept is a practical process ready for you to implement today.

We're not just offering you a guide; we're extending a hand to walk this journey with you. Inspired by the mentorship of R. Nelson Nash, we're eager to share this knowledge and experience with you. Your first step? A consultation with the right person on our team to understand your financial situation and tailor a program that aligns with your objectives and cash flow.

Are you ready to embark on this life-changing journey?

You should know how to use dividend-paying life insurance as a tool to implement this process

And you should have a great mentor who can show you how to build your Family Banking System.

We have a proven track record built on 16 years of experience. We pride ourselves on earning our clients' trust. You get our whole team to work with, lifetime coaching, and expertise for business owners. We understand what our clients truly value, and we provide it every day!

Many people are only one tiny little excuse away from taking a progressive step forward in their lives. Most people let procrastination cheat them out of great, big leaps of progress. The clients we love to serve are not most people!

Scheduling a conversation with us is your opportunity to:

- Discover personalized methods of implementing this process in your life

- Elevate your wealth-building journey

- Take the first step towards a bigger financial future

Start your Infinite Banking adventure now. Go to **DontSpreadWealth.com/bonus** and access all of the free video courses we've created for you!

Exercise: Write down the top five advantages you will have with your own family banking system.

1. _____
2. _____
3. _____
4. _____
5. _____

Let's build a future where financial freedom isn't just a dream but an achievable reality.

The time is now—let's make it happen together!

BONUS: Insights to Action Worksheet

To unlock the full potential of this book, your personal insights and reflections are key. This worksheet is all about diving deep into your own thoughts and reasons. It's your chance to truly grasp why creating a family banking system matters for you.

Dedicate some focused time to work through the following responses. This exercise will help you uncover the real value and impact of implementing this system in your life.

And if you prefer keeping this book pristine, don't worry! You can download the worksheet directly from your bonuses here: **DontSpreadWealth.com/bonus**.

Insights to Action

Take a moment to estimate how much money you have spent from your very first paycheck up to this point in your lifetime.

$ _____

Could you write a check for that amount of money right now?

Circle One: YES   NO

WHO did all the work to earn that money?

Circle One: I DID

WHO got all that money?

Circle One: SOMEONE ELSE

How much additional interest can you earn on all that money?

$ _____

Reflect on your responses above. How does that make you feel?

_____

_____

_____

_____

_____

_____

_____

You did all the work. Someone else got all your money. You can no longer earn interest on any of that money for the remainder of your lifetime and every generation that comes after you.

Is that a Problem?

Circle One: YES   NO

How soon do you want to begin solving your problem?

Circle One: NOW   NEVER

I chose NOW because ...

_____
_____
_____
_____
_____
_____

Think about the people in your family and/or business that you would do anything for. Write their names here.

_____
_____
_____
_____
_____
_____

Envision the advantages of having your own Family Banking System in place. How would this change your family and/or business's future?

_____

_____

_____

_____

_____

_____

Picture the day when you have complete control over HOW you finance all the things you need throughout your lifetime. How would this control impact the way you save, spend, and invest?

_____

_____

_____

_____

_____

_____

What kind of financial legacy do you wish to create within your family?

_____

_____

_____

_____

_____

_____

How can The Infinite Banking Concept help you achieve this legacy?

_____

_____

_____

_____

_____

_____

If we were having this discussion three years from today, and you were looking back over those three years to today, what specifically has to have happened in your life, both personally and professionally, in order for you to feel happy with your progress?

_____

_____

_____

_____

_____

_____

"To know and not to do ... is not to know."
– Chinese Proverb

Knowledge is made meaningful through action.

Recommended Reading

Other Books from Jayson Lowe and Richard Canfield

- *Cash Follows the Leader: Uninterrupted Daily Growth with High Cash Value Life Insurance*

- *Canadian's Guide to Wealth Building Without Risk: The Process of Becoming Your Own Banker*

- *Keep Taxes Away From Your Wealth: 5 Strategies for Reducing Taxes You Owe Now and Into the Future*

Books to help you think differently

Becoming Your Own Banker: Unlock the Infinite Banking Concept - R. Nelson Nash

Building Your Warehouse of Wealth: A Grassroots Method of Avoiding Fractional Reserve Banking—Think About It! - R. Nelson Nash

Who Not How - Dan Sullivan

The Gap and The Gain - Dan Sullivan

Epic Life - Justin Breen

The Case for IBC: How To Secede From Our Current Monetary Regime One Household At A Time - R. Nelson Nash, L. Carlos Lara, Robert P. Murphy PhD

The Perfect Investment: Understanding Whole Life Insurance Nelson Nash's Infinite Banking Concept - L. Carlos Lara

About the Authors

Jayson Lowe is the founder of The Lowe Group of Companies, including the Wealth Without Bay Street Podcast and Ascendant Financial Inc. A visionary and a gifted leader, he has over 22 years of experience as a highly regarded coach, speaker, and advisor to individuals and business owners nationwide.

When he's not building the Ascendant Financial organization he owns with his wife, Rebecca, Jayson enjoys spending quality time with his four children.

Richard Canfield is an Authorized Infinite Banking Practitioner and co-host of the Wealth Without Bay Street Podcast. He is passionate about helping families take more control over their financial lives.

When not helping others, Richard enjoys spending time with his two kids and his amazing wife, Heather. He loves the mountains, time at the lake/beach, anything with a zipline, and busting out tools for random household projects. He thrives to learn new things and always seeks personal growth.

CONNECT WITH JAYSON

Follow him on your favorite
social media platforms today.

WealthWithoutBayStreet.com/YouTube

UNLOCK THE SECRETS TO CREATING FINANCIAL PEACE OF MIND IN AN UNCERTAIN WORLD

KEYNOTE SPEAKERS

START THE CONVERSATION TODAY

WealthWithoutBayStreet.com/Keynote

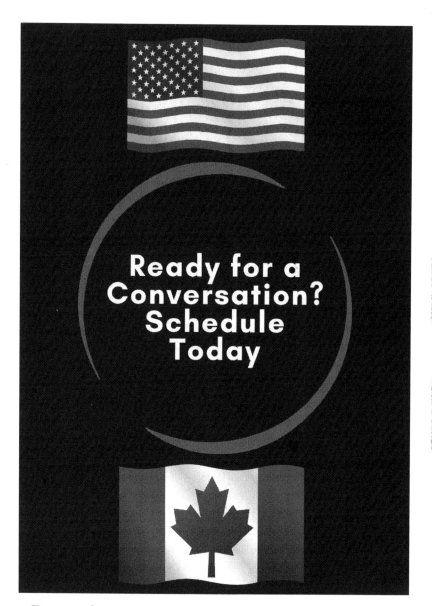

DontSpreadWealth.com/bonus

ACCESS OUR FAMILY BANKING SYSTEM RESOURCES ANYTIME!

AVAILABLE ON THE HOUSE AT NO CHARGE!

DontSpreadWealth.com/bonus

Add These Books To Your Wealth Building Library

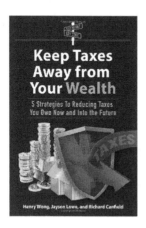

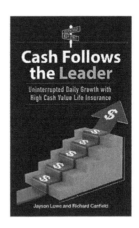

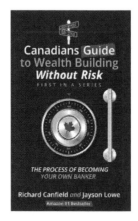

AVAILABLE WHEREVER BOOKS ARE SOLD

THIS BOOK IS PROTECTED INTELLECTUAL PROPERTY

The author of this book values Intellectual Property. The book you just read is protected by Easy IP®, a proprietary process, which integrates blockchain technology giving Intellectual Property "Global Protection." By creating a "Time-Stamped" smart contract that can never be tampered with or changed, we establish "First Use" that tracks back to the author.

Easy IP® functions much like a Pre-Patent™ since it provides an immutable "First Use" of the Intellectual Property. This is achieved through our proprietary process of leveraging blockchain technology and smart contracts. As a result, proving "First Use" is simple through a global and verifiable smart contract. By protecting intellectual property with blockchain technology and smart contracts, we establish a "First to File" event.

Protected By Easy IP®

LEARN MORE AT EASYIP.TODAY